JOHN F. KENNEDY
(1917–1963)

QUOTATIONS

OF

John F. Kennedy

APPLEWOOD BOOKS
Bedford, Massachusetts

John F. Kennedy

JOHN FITZGERALD KENNEDY was born in Brookline, Massachusetts, on May 29, 1917, the second of nine children born to Joseph P. and Rose Fitzgerald Kennedy. After graduating from Harvard in 1940, Kennedy enlisted in the U.S. Navy and was eventually assigned to the South Pacific as commander of a patrol torpedo boat. He received a Purple Heart and the Navy and Marine Corps Medal for leading survivors to safety after his boat was sunk by a Japanese destroyer.

In 1946, Kennedy was elected congressman from Massachusetts and went on to serve three terms in the U.S. House of Representatives. In 1952, Kennedy narrowly defeated Henry Cabot Lodge Jr. to become U.S. senator. He married Jacqueline Bouvier in September 1953. The couple had three children, two of whom survived childhood.

After undergoing multiple back surgeries, Kennedy wrote *Profiles in Courage* during his convalescence. The book, published in 1956, became a bestseller and won the Pulitzer Prize for biography the following year.

In 1960, Kennedy was elected president of the United States, defeating Richard M. Nixon by a narrow margin. At the age of forty-three, he became the youngest man and the first

Catholic ever to be elected president.

At his inauguration in 1961, Kennedy urged his fellow Americans to "ask not what your country can do for you—ask what you can do for your country." In that spirit, he established the Peace Corps to promote cultural understanding and to provide support to developing countries. During his presidency, the White House became the cultural center of the nation, with the first couple hosting artists, musicians, and writers. The Kennedy administration addressed civil rights violence by sending troops to both the University of Mississippi and the University of Alabama to restore order and desegregate the schools. Kennedy's administration made space a national priority by setting the goal of having man land on the moon before 1970. Early in his presidency, Kennedy attempted to overthrow the Communist Castro government in Cuba by sponsoring the failed Bay of Pigs invasion. Later, in a defining moment of his presidency, the world came to the brink of nuclear war during the Cuban missile crisis. The crisis was averted when the Soviets withdrew their nuclear arms.

As his last major action as president, Kennedy called for the biggest income tax cut in U.S. history in an effort to strengthen the economy, and sent the most comprehensive and far-reaching civil rights bill to Congress in 1963. On the morning of November 22, 1963, President Kennedy was assassinated in Dallas, Texas.

QUOTATIONS
OF
John F. Kennedy

I look forward to an America which will not be afraid of grace and beauty, which will protect the beauty of our natural environment, which will preserve the great old American houses and squares and parks of our national past and which will build handsome and balanced cities for our future.

John F. Kennedy

*A*rt is the great democrat, calling forth creative genius from every sector of society, disregarding race or religion or wealth or color.

John F. Kennedy

*W*e must never forget that art is not a form of propaganda; it is a form of truth.

John F. Kennedy

*W*hen power leads man toward arrogance, poetry reminds him of his limitations. When power narrows the area of man's concern, poetry reminds him of the richness and diversity of existence. When power corrupts, poetry cleanses.

There are three things in life which are real: God, human folly and laughter. Since the first two are beyond our comprehension, we must do what we can with the third.

John F. Kennedy

I look forward to an America which will reward achievement in the arts as we reward achievement in business or statecraft.

John F. Kennedy

The Supreme Reality of Our Time is...the common vulnerability of this planet.

John F. Kennedy

Thus it is our task in our time and in our generation to hand down undiminished to those who come after us, as was handed down to us by those who went before, the natural wealth and beauty which is ours.

*L*et both sides seek to invoke the wonders of science instead of its terrors. Together let us explore the stars, conquer the deserts, eradicate disease, tap the ocean depths, and encourage the arts and commerce.

John F. Kennedy

*W*e choose to go to the moon, not because it's easy but because it's hard. We choose to go to the moon in this decade and do the other things, not because they are easy but because they are hard…

John F. Kennedy

*F*irst, I believe that this nation should commit itself to achieving the goal, before this decade is out, of landing a man on the moon and returning him safely to earth.

I really don't know why it is that all of us
are so committed to the sea, except I think
it's because in addition to the fact that the
sea changes, and the light changes, and ships
change, it's because we all came from the sea.
And it is an interesting biological fact that all
of us have in our veins the exact same percent-
age of salt in our blood that exists in the ocean,
and, therefore, we have salt in our blood, in
our sweat, and in our tears. We are tied to
the ocean. And when we go back to the sea,
whether it is to sail or to watch it, we are going
back from whence we came.

John F. Kennedy

*B*ut in a very real sense, it will not be one
man going to the moon if we make this judgment affirmatively, it will be an entire nation.
For all of us must work to put him there.

John F. Kennedy

*T*he greater our knowledge increases the more
our ignorance unfolds.

*F*or the great enemy of the truth is very often not the lie—deliberate, contrived and dishonest, but the myth, persistent, persuasive, and unrealistic. We enjoy the comfort of opinion without the discomfort of thought.

John F. Kennedy

I think this is the most extraordinary collection of talent, of human knowledge, that has ever been gathered at the White House—with the possible exception of when Thomas Jefferson dined alone.
[Describing a dinner for Nobel Prize winners]

John F. Kennedy

*L*et us think of education as the means of developing our greatest abilities, because in each of us there is a private hope and dream which, fulfilled, can be translated into benefit for everyone and greater strength for our nation.

*F*or education...is the mainspring of our economic and social progress...it is the highest expression of achievement in our society, ennobling and enriching human life.

John F. Kennedy

*F*or liberty without learning is always in peril; and learning without liberty is always in vain.

John F. Kennedy

*O*ur progress as a nation can be no swifter than our progress in education. The human mind is our fundamental resource.

John F. Kennedy

*O*ur deep spiritual confidence that this nation will survive the perils of today...compels us to invest in our nation's future, to consider and meet our obligations to our children and the numberless generations that will follow.

*M*odern cynics and skeptics... see no harm in paying those to whom they entrust the minds of their children a smaller wage than is paid to those to whom they entrust the care of their plumbing.

John F. Kennedy

A child miseducated is a child lost.

John F. Kennedy

*M*an is still the most extraordinary computer of all.

John F. Kennedy

*A*ll of us do not have equal talent, but all of us should have an equal opportunity to develop those talents.

John F. Kennedy

*I*t might be said now that I have the best of both worlds: a Harvard education and a Yale degree.

The Chinese use two brush strokes to write the word 'crisis.' One brush stroke stands for danger; the other for opportunity. In a crisis, be aware of the danger—but recognize the opportunity.

John F. Kennedy

Things do not happen. Things are made to happen.

John F. Kennedy

Do not pray for easy lives. Pray to be stronger men.

John F. Kennedy

A man does what he must—in spite of personal consequences, in spite of obstacles and dangers and pressures—and that is the basis of all human morality.

John F. Kennedy

Great crises produce great men, and great deeds of courage.

What really counts is not the immediate act of courage or of valor, but those who bear the struggle day in and day out—not the sunshine patriots but those who are willing to stand for a long period of time.

John F. Kennedy

Truth is a tyrant—the only tyrant to whom we can give our allegiance. The service of truth is a matter of heroism.

John F. Kennedy

The stories of past courage can define that ingredient—they can teach, they can offer hope, they can provide inspiration. But they cannot supply courage itself. For this each man must look into his own soul.

John F. Kennedy

I am certain that after the dust of centuries has passed over our cities, we, too, will be remembered not for victories or defeats in battle or in politics but for our contributions to the human spirit.

A nation which has forgotten the quality of courage which in the past has been brought to public life is not as likely to insist upon or regard that quality in its chosen leaders today— and in fact we have forgotten.

John F. Kennedy

A s we express our gratitude, we must never forget that the highest appreciation is not to utter words, but to live by them.

John F. Kennedy

I am not the Catholic candidate for President. I am the Democratic Party's candidate for President, who happens also to be a Catholic.

John F. Kennedy

I t would be premature to ask your support in the next election and it would be inaccurate to thank you for it in the past.

*T*o exclude from positions of trust and command all those below the age of 44 would have kept Jefferson from writing the Declaration of Independence, Washington from commanding the Continental Army, Madison from fathering the Constitution, Hamilton from serving as secretary of the treasury, Clay from being elected speaker of the House and Christopher Columbus from discovering America.

John F. Kennedy

*I*t has recently been suggested that whether I serve one or two terms in the Presidency, I will find myself at the end of that period at what might be called the awkward age, too old to begin a new career and too young to write my memoirs.

John F. Kennedy

I would rather be accused of breaking precedents than breaking promises.

Governments can err, Presidents do make mistakes, but the immortal Dante tells us that divine justice weighs the sins of the cold-blooded and the sins of the warm-hearted on different scales. Better the occasional faults of a party living in the spirit of charity than the consistent omissions of a party frozen in the ice of its own indifference.

John F. Kennedy

Senators who go down to defeat in a vain defense of a single principle will not be on hand to fight for that or any other principle in the future.

John F. Kennedy

My experience in government is that when things are non-controversial, beautifully coordinated, and all the rest it may be that there isn't much going on.

John F. Kennedy

Those who make peaceful revolution impossible will make violent revolution inevitable.

*A*nd our duty as a party is not to our party alone, but to the nation and, indeed, to all mankind. Our duty is not merely the preservation of political power but the preservation of peace and freedom.

John F. Kennedy

*F*or the unity of freedom has never relied on uniformity of opinion.

John F. Kennedy

*T*he men who create power make an indispensable contribution to the Nation's greatness, but the men who question power make a contribution just as indispensable, especially when that questioning is disinterested, for they determine whether we use power or power uses us.

John F. Kennedy

*T*here will always be dissident voices heard in the land, expressing opposition without alternatives, finding fault but never favor, perceiving gloom on every side and seeking influence without responsibility.

*M*ankind must put an end to war or war will put an end to mankind.

John F. Kennedy

*U*nconditional war can no longer lead to unconditional victory. It can no longer serve to settle disputes... It can no longer concern the great powers alone.

John F. Kennedy

*T*he basic problems facing the world today are not susceptible to a military solution.

John F. Kennedy

*F*or a nation that is afraid to let its people judge the truth and falsehood in an open market is a nation that is afraid of its people.

John F. Kennedy

*W*ar will exist until that distant day when the conscientious objector enjoys the same reputation and prestige that the warrior does today.

$\mathcal{A}$ll this will not be finished in the first one hundred days. Nor will it be finished in the first one thousand days, nor in the life of this administration, nor even perhaps in our lifetime on this planet. But let us begin.

John F. Kennedy

$\mathcal{S}$o let us begin anew—remembering on both sides that civility is not a sign of weakness, and sincerity is always subject to proof. Let us never negotiate out of fear. But let us never fear to negotiate.

John F. Kennedy

$\mathcal{T}$he essential fact that both of these groups fail to grasp is that diplomacy and defense are not substitutes for one another. Either alone will fail.

John F. Kennedy

$\mathcal{D}$omestic policy can only defeat us; foreign policy can kill us.

*F*or the purpose of foreign policy is not to provide an outlet for our own sentiments of hope or indignation; it is to shape real events in a real world.

John F. Kennedy

*O*ur goal is not the victory of might, but the vindication of right—not peace at the expense of freedom, but both peace and freedom, here in this hemisphere, and, we hope, around the world. God willing, that goal will be achieved.

John F. Kennedy

*W*e cannot expect that all nations will adopt like systems, for conformity is the jailer of freedom and the enemy of growth.

John F. Kennedy

*W*e shall be judged more by what we do at home than by what we preach abroad.

John F. Kennedy

*F*or we prefer world law in the age of self-determination to world war in the age of mass extermination.

*A*cting on our own, by ourselves, we cannot establish justice throughout the world... But joined with other free nations... we can assist the developing nations to throw off the yoke of poverty.

John F. Kennedy

*T*he United States is a peaceful nation. And where our strength and determination are clear, our words need merely to convey conviction, not belligerence. If we are strong, our strength will speak for itself. If we are weak, words will be of no help.

John F. Kennedy

*W*hat kind of peace do we seek? Not a Pax Americana enforced on the world by American weapons of war. Not the peace of the grave or the security of the slave. I am talking about genuine peace, the kind of peace that makes life on earth worth living...not merely peace for Americans, but peace for all men and women; not merely peace in our time, but peace for all time.

I look forward to a great future for America —a future in which our country will match its military strength with our moral restraint, its wealth with our wisdom, its power with our purpose.

John F. Kennedy

*A*nd we must face the fact that the United States is neither omnipotent or omniscient —that we are only six percent of the world's population—that we cannot impose our will upon the other ninety-four percent of mankind —that we cannot right every wrong or reverse each adversity—and that therefore there cannot be an American solution to every world problem.

John F. Kennedy

*P*olitical sovereignty is but a mockery without the means of meeting poverty and illiteracy and disease. Self-determination is but a slogan if the future holds no hope.

John F. Kennedy

*I*f a free society cannot help the many who are poor, it cannot save the few who are rich.

*D*emocracy is never a final achievement. It is a call to effort, to sacrifice, and a willingness to live and to die in its defense.

John F. Kennedy

*L*et every nation know, whether it wishes us well or ill, that we shall pay any price, bear any burden, meet any hardship, support any friend, oppose any foe to assure the survival and the success of liberty.

John F. Kennedy

*F*or in the final analysis, our most basic common link, is that we all inhabit this small planet, we all breathe the same air, we all cherish our children's futures, and we are all mortal.

John F. Kennedy

*E*conomic growth without social progress lets the great majority of the people remain in poverty, while a privileged few reap the benefits of rising abundance.

The world is very different now. For man holds in his mortal hands the power to abolish all forms of human poverty, and all forms of human life.

John F. Kennedy

Never before has man had such capacity to control his own environment, to end thirst and hunger, to conquer poverty and disease, to banish illiteracy and massive human misery... We have the power to make this the best generation of mankind in the history of the world—or to make it the last.

John F. Kennedy

Economic policy can result from governmental inaction as well as governmental action.

John F. Kennedy

There is inherited wealth in this country and also inherited poverty.

A strong America depends on its cities— America's glory and sometimes America's shame.

John F. Kennedy

W e will neglect our cities at our peril, for in neglecting them we neglect the nation.

John F. Kennedy

W herever we are, we must all, in our daily lives, live up to the age-old faith that peace and freedom walk together. In too many of our cities today, the peace is not secure because freedom is incomplete.

John F. Kennedy

T he quality of American life must keep pace with the quantity of American goods. This country cannot afford to be materially rich and spiritually poor.

*F*or one true measure of a nation is its success in fulfilling the promise of a better life for each of its members. Let this be the measure of our nation.

John F. Kennedy

*N*ow the trumpet summons us again—not as a call to bear arms, though arms we need—not as a call to battle, though embattled we are— but a call to bear the burden of a long twilight struggle year in and year out 'rejoicing in hope, patient in tribulation'—a struggle against the common enemies of man: tyranny, poverty, disease and war itself.

John F. Kennedy

I want every American free to stand up for his rights, even if sometimes he has to sit down for them.

John F. Kennedy

*O*ur problems are man-made; therefore they can be solved by man. No problem of human destiny is beyond human beings.

...*U*nless there is the most intimate association between those who look to the far horizons and those who deal with our daily problems, then...we shall not pass through these stormy times with success.

John F. Kennedy

*W*hen at some future date the high court of history sits in judgment on each one of us- recording whether in our brief span of service we fulfilled our responsibilities to the state— our success or failure, in whatever office we may hold, will be measured by the answers to four questions—were we truly men of courage ... were we truly men of judgment ... were we truly men of integrity ... were we truly men of dedication?

John F. Kennedy

*A*nd so, my fellow Americans: ask not what your country can do for you—ask what you can do for your country. My fellow citizens of the world: ask not what America will do for you, but what together we can do for the freedom of man.

This is a great country and requires a good deal of all of us, so I can imagine nothing more important than for all of you to continue to work in public affairs and be interested in them, not only to bring up a family, but also give part of your time to your community, your state, and your country.

John F. Kennedy

We stand today on the edge of a new frontier...The new frontier of which I speak is not a set of promises—it is a set of challenges. It sums up not what I intend to offer the American people, but what I intend to ask of them....It appeals to our pride, not to their pocketbook—it holds out the promise of more sacrifice instead of more security.

John F. Kennedy

The problems of the world cannot possibly be solved by skeptics or cynics whose horizons are limited by the obvious realities. We need men who can dream of things that never were...and ask why not.

... *I* look forward to an America which commands respect throughout the world, not only for its strength, but for its civilization as well. And I look forward to a world which will be safe not only for democracy and diversity but also for personal distinction.

John F. Kennedy

We celebrate the past to awaken the future.

John F. Kennedy

We dare not forget that we are the heirs of that first revolution.

John F. Kennedy

This nation was founded by men of many nations and backgrounds. It was founded on the principle that all men are created equal and that the rights of every man are diminished when the rights of one man are threatened.

$\mathcal{F}$or I can assure you that we love our country, not for what it was, though it has always been great...not for what it is, though of this we are deeply proud...but for what it someday can, and, through the effort of us all, someday will be.

John F. Kennedy

$\mathcal{T}$he true democracy, living and growing and inspiring, puts its faith in the people - faith that the people will not simply elect men who will represent their views ably and faithfully, but will also elect men who will exercise their con-scientious judgment—faith that the people will not condemn those whose devotion to prin-ciple leads them to unpopular courses, but will reward courage, respect honor, and ultimately recognize right.

John F. Kennedy

$\mathcal{P}$eace is a daily, a weekly, a monthly process, gradually changing opinions, slowly eroding old barriers, quietly building new structures.